Invitation To Love:
Celebrating the Love Poems
of
Paul Laurence Dunbar

Paul Laurence Dunbar

Introduction and Edited by
Rhonda Rhea, J.D., M.Div.

Copyright, 2007, 2016

Published By
J S Publishing, LLC
www.jspublishing.me
ISBN-13 978-0-9795060-0-0
ISBN-10 0-9795060-0-x

Dedication

This book is dedicated to love and to all of the people who believe in the power of love.
To my mother, the late Dr. Marlene Rhea for loving me and introducing me to the poetry of Paul Laurence Dunbar.
To my son Carson who has taught me about unconditional love.

In Memory of Lottie S. Knight
Hampton University

Love

*If I speak in the tongues of men and of angels,
but have not love,
I am only a resounding gong or a clanging cymbal.*

*If I have the gift of prophecy and can fathom all mysteries
and all knowledge, and if I have a faith
that can move mountains, but have not love,
I am nothing.*

*If I give all I possess to the poor and surrender my body to
the flames, but have not love,
I gain nothing.*

*Love is patient, love is kind. It does not envy, it does not
boast, it is not proud. It is not rude, it is not self-seeking,
it is not easily angered, it keeps no record of wrongs.
Love does not delight in evil but rejoices with the truth.
It always protects, always trusts, always hopes,
always perseveres.
Love never fails...*

*And now these three remain: faith, hope and love. But the
greatest of these is love.*

I Corinthians 13:1-8,13

Table of Contents

Acknowledgements i
Introduction iii

The Poems of Paul Laurence Dunbar
Intimate Love

Alice	3
The Phantom Kiss	4
Waiting	6
If	8
Invitation To Love	9
Longing	10
She Gave Me A Rose	11
Morning	12
To Her	13
Love's Apotheosis	14
Suppose	16
Love-Song	17
Nora: A Serenade	18
Dream Song I	19
A Bridal Measure	20
The Awakening	21
To A Lady Playing The Harp	22
A Love Song	24
Morning Song of Love	25
Night of Love	26
Roses and Pearls	27
Come and Kiss Me Twenty	28
Howe Should I Woo Thee	30

Table of Contents, continued

Defining Love

The Master-Player	33
A Question	33
Kidnapped	34
Love	35
Love Despoiled	36
Love's Phases	37
A Lyric	38
The Quilting	39
Confirmation	39
The Wooing	40
My Little March Girl	42
Her Thought and His	43
The Disturber	44
Dinah Kneading Dough	46
Love's Castle	47
Love's Seasons	48
Two Songs	49
Passion and Love	50

Losing Love

My Love Irene	53
Ballard	54
Ships That Pass in the Night	55
Lyrics of Love and Sorrow	56
Love's Draft	59

Table of Contents, continued

A Golden Day 60
Then and Now 61
Yesterday and To-Morrow 62
Love and Grief 63
If I Could But Forget 64

Humorous Love

A Made To Order Smile 67
A Negro Love Song 68
The Photograph 69
Discovered 70
A Love Letter 71
Angelina 72
Parted 73
The Looking-Glass 74
A Plea 75
Howdy Honey Howdy 76
My Sweet Brown Gal 77

Bibliography

Acknowledgements

I would like to thank God for his faithfulness, always and for giving me the strength to complete this project.

I would like to acknowledge the following individuals who have given so much to me. First of all to my sister, Monica for your love and for always encouraging me to follow my dreams. To my niece, Rhea who loves me so much, thanks for always listening and laughing. To my late father, James, thanks for your love and interest in this project. To my late grandparents, Grace and Hurley Covington who gave so much to me. To my late grandmother, Alma Woodruff, my absolute best friend in the whole wide world, I love you!

Many, many thanks to the Dunbar House. You provide such an invaluable service to so many people by keeping the poetry and the memory of Paul Laurence Dunbar alive.

To all of my family and friends, I appreciate you.

My Journey

As a child growing up in Dayton, Ohio I was always familiar with the poetry of Paul Laurence Dunbar. My mother loved his poems and made it a point that my sister and I would know about Dunbar as well. We would often drive by his house on then Summit Street and my mother would remind us over and over again that we were riding past the home of Black America's greatest writer, Paul Laurence Dunbar.

About ten years ago I had the opportunity to meet Mrs. Laverne Sci, the curator of the Dunbar House. We were both participants at a Black History event and during the course of our meeting we began a conversation about Paul Laurence Dunbar. Immediately following the event, Mrs. Sci invited me to stop by the Dunbar House for another Black History program.

I began to volunteer and participate in events at the Dunbar House. In my childhood, a visit to the Dunbar House was always a standard school field trip. I was familiar with some of Dunbar's poetry. Everyone was required in school or in church to memorize "In the Morning". I had this sense of pride and a belief that I really "knew" the poetry of Paul Laurence Dunbar.

As the fall season began, Mrs. Sci approached me about writing the annual Dunbar House Christmas play. This annual play allowed local writers, actors and actresses to pool their collective talents, and for a series of week-ends, bring the Dunbar House to life. Visitors were given private tours which included live performances of Dunbar's poetry in each room of the house. Because I am a trained writer, I could not begin my own efforts until I had the opportunity to study and get to know Dunbar on his own terms. I took the collection of poems homes and I became absorbed. I read the entire collection over and over again. I was not able to write until I could feel his presence in my own spirit.

I produced a play, "Christmas Late in De'Eve'n" and it was well received by the public. I presented different Dunbar material that had not been introduced in past plays. As I was turning in my script I said to Mrs. Sci and to her assistant Gerry Primm, "You know Mrs. Sci, this is a really good script and we can go a lot of places with this play but have you ever looked at his love poems?"

In the course of my preparation for the Christmas play, I discovered in a sense, Paul Laurence Dunbar's love poems and I was speechless. I immediately began to engage Mrs. Sci into allowing me to have a Valentine's Day Dinner party, the first ever in the history of the Dunbar House. On Valentine's Day of the new year, Dunbar's love poems were performed in a live jazz setting. The intimacy was indescribable. The dinner was not just about the simple fulfillment for the day. Yes, we were all individuals who shared a common love of Paul Laurence Dunbar's work. But we also understood that this was a greater call. That Valentine's Day dinner was about giving Dunbar honor. We were giving him a voice that had been silenced. We were giving him identity as a man.

It has taken me a while to come back to Dunbar. My own life experiences have helped me to see him with a different set of eyes. I am honored to be the vessel to bring this body of work to you.

Paul Laurence Dunbar was such a prolific writer who was often misunderstood and not celebrated in totality. It is through this collection of love poems, that one has the opportunity to see another dimension to Dunbar. "Invitation to Love" is one of my favorite Paul Laurence Dunbar's love poems and it is the inspiration for this book.

Love is the universal and often unspoken need that is sought and desired by everyone. This compilation of poetry gives us the many facets of love. It tells of the intimacy of love; the betrayal of love; the humor in love; and the definition of love.

The poems contained in this book are mostly written in standard English. There are a only few poems that are written in dialect, the language in which Dunbar was most celebrated.

This project is historic in nature. It is the one of the first times that Paul Laurence Dunbar's love poems have been complied as one body of work and presented for public enjoyment. One of the most significant aspects of this collection rest in the fact that the poems presented here are more than one hundred years old. Yet, as you read through the pages, you will find the poems to be timeless. This is especially noteworthy because during Dunbar's lifetime, most of these poems were unknown and certainly not celebrated.

Because of the racial climate in which Dunbar lived, he was limited publicly as an writer. He toured all over the world, reciting his poetry. The world grew to know him as "the Negro poet". And in that definition, Paul Laurence Dunbar became synonymous with the dialect form of writing. He was often the center of controversy, particularly in the African American community. As much as he was celebrated for his accomplishments in poetry and in writing, he was equally resented for keeping that "old slave talk alive."

It is my hope that by reading the poems in this book, one can dispel the myth, particularly in looking at the African American community, that we don't know or experience intimate love. Paul Laurence Dunbar was a man who loved and loved deeply. Even though the era in which he lived imposed limitations on him as a man, this collection of poetry clearly exposes the depth of his being. Dunbar proves that love is blind: that in its purest form, love transcends all limitations and all barriers. Through this collection of poetry, Dunbar speaks in a timeless, universal language that is understood by all humankind.

Dunbar's Journey

Paul Laurence Dunbar was born on June 27, 1872 in Dayton, Ohio. His parents, Joshua and Matilda, were formerly enslaved. His father Joshua escaped from slavery. His mother, Matilda was freed from enslavement as a result of the Emancipation Proclamation. Paul's father Joshua, who wanted to fight against the injustice of slavery, served during the Civil War in the 55th Massachusetts Infantry Regiment and the 5th Massachusetts Colored Cavalry Regiment. His mother, Matilda was a laundress and did domestic work. His parents separated when Paul was young but they both instilled in him a desire to be educated. Both of his parents were self-taught. His mother Matilda loved poetry and shared this love of poetry with Paul. Paul began to write poems as early as six years old. He had his first poetry recital at the age of nine.

Dunbar attended an all-white high school. His high school friends were Wilbur and Orville Wright, now famous for their contributions to aviation. They owned a printing press and published some of Dunbar's first work. Professionally, Dunbar desired to become a lawyer. He was unable to fulfill this dream due the racial conditions of the time. Poetry became the vehicle for Dunbar's fame.

Paul Laurence Dunbar worked as an elevator operator at the Callahan Building in Dayton, Ohio. While riding up and down between floors, Dunbar was able to perfect his craft. He would often read his poetry to the elevator passengers. In 1893, Dunbar published his first collection of poetry, *Oak and Ivy* at his own expense. His second collection of poetry, *Majors and Minors*, was financed by Dr. Henry Archibald Tobey, a physician who had befriend Dunbar. Dr. Tobey circulated this collection of poetry among his friends. Eventually, Dunbar's poetry caught the attention of William Dean Howells, of *Harper's Weekly* magazine. This was the breakthrough that Dunbar had long sought. It appear that almost overnight, Paul Laurence Dunbar was known through out the world.

Dunbar traveled throughout Europe and the United States reciting his poetry. He was a great orator, as well. Dunbar's contribution to literature was not just limited to poetry. He was a writer of many genre. Dunbar's fame allowed him to travel in the elite circles with Fredrick Douglas, Booker T. Washington and other influential people of that time.

In March, 1898, Dunbar married Alice Ruth Moore, a fellow poet and school teacher. They had corresponded with one another for two years before they met and married. In many reports, their relationship was at times turbulent, however, as this collection of poems reflect, their love for one another was unquestionable. They had a love story.

Dunbar saw a picture of Alice Ruth Moore in a magazine that had published her poetry. Dunbar took a notion to write her a letter. Alice Ruth Moore responded and Dunbar fell instantly in love.

It is reported that her parents were opposed to their relationship. Alice Ruth Moore was of a middle-class background. Dunbar was not. Paul was scheduled to depart for Europe and the intensity of their relationship had grown to an unbearable stage. They had never physically met, yet they knew their love for one another was certain. Against her parents wishes, Alice Ruth Moore ran away to meet Dunbar prior to his departure to Europe. He was surprise to see her at his farewell party but he knew that this was his wife and that night, using his mother's wedding ring, Paul Laurence Dunbar proposed to Miss Alice Ruth Moore. They eloped upon his return from Europe.

Paul Laurence Dunbar suffered from tuberculosis for many years. When the doctors could find no cure, Dunbar turned to his own remedies. Eventually, Dunbar's found a tonic containing alcohol could relieve the pain of coughing. As a result of his poor health and alcohol dependency, his marriage ended in 1902. Dunbar return to Dayton, Ohio where he died on February 9, 1906. He was just thirty-three years old.

In just thirty-three short years, Paul Laurence Dunbar managed to become the first African American writer to achieve international acclaim and recognition. His contribution to literature included 12 books of poetry, four books of short stories, a play and five novels. He contributed to countless journals, newspapers and magazines.

Paul Laurence Dunbar was a man who knew love. He loved his mother, Matilda with much honor and devotion. He loved Alice Ruth Moore with a deep intensity. He loved his friends and he loved his affair with the written word.

Your Journey

In the universe of life, there are no accidents. We each are guided by Divine Providence. So it is no accident that you have this book. Whether given as a gift or a purchase, it is my hope that this collection of poetry will enlighten your soul and awaken in you the gift of love.

Paul Laurence Dunbar was such a literary genius. He had a unique way to pull you in. As you read these poems you will hear them come alive. You too, will feel them in your soul. In your spirit you will celebrate the unveiling of perhaps, one of this phenomenal writer's greatest gifts to us: this collection of love poems which have been silently tucked away and hidden, until now. This collection of poetry gives Dunbar a new identity and definition, as a man. It allows us the opportunity to peak into his inner most thoughts and feelings about love.

Thank you for taking this journey with me and for experiencing this renaissance: a true rebirth of love.

Intimate Love

The poems in this section reflect some of Paul Laurence Dunbar's most intimate and personal thoughts about love. Many of the poems are pleading in nature and seem to ask the question, "What must I do to win your love?" There are several poems that should be considered classics: "How Should I Woo Thee"; "Love's Apotheosis"; and "Invitation to Love".

Alice

KNOW you, winds that blow your course
Down the verdant valleys,
That somewhere you must, perforce,
Kiss the brow of Alice?
When her gentle face you find,
Kiss it softly, naughty wind.
Roses waving fair and sweet
Thro' the garden alleys,
Grow into a glory meet
For the eye of Alice;
Let the wind your offering bear
Of sweet perfume, faint and rare.
Lily holding crystal dew
In your pure white chalice,
Nature kind hath fashioned you
Like the soul of Alice;
It of purest white is wrought,
Filled with gems of crystal thought.

The Phantom Kiss

One night in my room, still and beamless,
With will and with thought in eclipse,
I rested in sleep that was dreamless;
When softly there fell on my lips

A touch, as of lips that were pressing
Mine own with the message of bliss—
A sudden, soft, fleeting caressing,
A breath like a maiden's first kiss.

I woke—and the scoffer may doubt me—
I peered in surprise through the gloom;
But nothing and none were about me,
And I was alone in my room.

Invitation to Love

Perhaps 't was the wind that caressed me
And touched me with dew-laden breath;
Or, maybe, close-sweeping, there passed me
The low-winging Angel of Death.

Some sceptic may choose to disdain it,
Or one feign to read it aright,
Or wisdom may seek to explain it—
This mystical kiss in the night.

But rather let fancy thus clear it:
That, thinking of me here alone,
The miles were made naught, and, in spirit,
Thy lips, love, were laid on mine own.

Invitation to Love

Waiting

The sun has slipped his tether
    And galloped down the west.
(Oh, it's weary, weary waiting, love.)
The little bird is sleeping
    In the softness of its nest.
Night follows day, day follows dawn,
And so the time has come and gone:
    And it's weary, weary waiting, love.

The cruel wind is rising
    With a whistle and a wail.
(And it's weary, weary waiting, love.)
My eyes are seaward straining
    For the coming of a sail;
But void the sea, and void the beach
Far and beyond where gaze can reach!
    And it's weary, weary waiting, love.

Invitation to Love

I heard the bell-buoy ringing—
    How long ago it seems!
(Oh, it's weary, weary waiting, love.)
And ever still, its knelling
    Crashes in upon my dreams.
The banns were read, my frock was sewn;
Since then two seasons' winds have blown—
    And it's weary, weary waiting, love.

The stretches of the ocean
    Are bare and bleak to-day.
(Oh, it's weary, weary waiting, love.)
My eyes are growing dimmer—
    Is it tears, or age, or spray?
But I will stay till you come home.
Strange ships come in across the foam!
    But it's weary, weary waiting, love.

If

IF life were but a dream, my Love,
  And death the waking time;
If day had not a beam, my Love,
  And night had not a rhyme,—
A barren, barren world were this
Without one saving gleam -
I'd only ask that with a kiss
You'd wake me from the dream.

If dreaming were the sum of days,
  And loving were the bane;
If battling for a wreath of bays
  Could soothe a heart in pain,—
I'd scorn the meed of battle's might,
All other aims above
I'd choose the human's higher right,
To suffer and to love!

Invitation to Love

Invitation To Love

Come when the nights are bright with stars
    Or when the moon is mellow;
Come when the sun his golden bars
    Drops on the hay-field yellow.
Come in the twilight soft and gray,
Come in the night or come in the day,
Come, O Love, whene'er you may,
    And you are welcome, welcome.

You are sweet, O Love, dear Love,
You are soft as the nesting dove.
Come to my heart and bring it rest
As the bird flies home to its welcome nest.

Come when my heart is full of grief
    Or when my heart is merry;
Come with the falling of the leaf
    Or with the redd'ning cherry.
Come when the year's first blossom blows,
Come when the summer gleams and glows,
Come with the winter's drifting snows,
    And you are welcome, welcome.

Longing

If you could sit with me beside the sea to-day,
And whisper with me sweetest dreamings o'er and o'er;
I think I should not find the clouds so dim and gray,
And not so loud the waves complaining at the shore.

If you could sit with me upon the shore to-day,
And hold my hand in yours as in the days of old,
I think I should not mind the chill baptismal spray,
Nor fine my hand and heart and all the world so cold.

If you could walk with me upon the strand to-day,
And tell me that my longing love had won your own,
I think all my sad thoughts would then be put away,
And I could give back laughter for the Ocean's moan!

Invitation to Love

She Gave Me A Rose

She gave me a rose,
    And I kissed it and pressed it.
I love her, she knows,
    And my action confessed it.
She gave me a rose,
    And I kissed it and pressed it.

Ah, how my heart glows,
    Could I ever have guessed it?
It is fair to suppose
    That I might have repressed it:
She gave me a rose,
    And I kissed it and pressed it.

'T was a rhyme in life's prose
    That uplifted and blest it.
Man's nature, who knows
    Until love comes to test it?
She gave me a rose,
    And I kissed and pressed it.

Invitation to Love

Morning

The mist has left the greening plain,
The dew-drops shine like fairy rain,
The couquette rose awakes again
    Her lovely self adorning.
The Wind is hiding in the trees,
A sighing, soothing, laughing tease,
Until the rose says "Kiss me, please,"
'Tis morning, 'tis morning.

With staff in hand and careless-free,
The wanderer fares right jauntily,
For towns and houses are, thinks he,
    For scorning, for scorning.
My soul is swift upon the wing,
And in its deeps a song I bring;
Come, Love, and we together sing,
" 'Tis morning, 'tis morning."

To Her

Your presence like a benison to me
    Wakes my sick soul to dreamful ecstasy,
I fancy that some old Arabian night
Saw you my houri and my heart's delight.

And wanderin forth beneath the passionate moon,
    Your love-strung zither and my soul in tune,
We knew the joy, the haunting of the pain
    That like a flame thrills through me now again.

To-night we sit where sweet the spice winds blow,
    A wind the northland lacks and ne'er shall know,
With clasped hands and spirits all aglow
    As in Arabia in the long ago.

Invitation to Love

Love's Apotheosis

Love me. I care not what the circling years
    To me may do.
If, but in spite of time and tears,
    You prove but true.

Love me – albeit grief shall dim mine eyes,
    And tears bedew,
I shall not e'en complain, for then my skies
    Shall still be blue.

Love me, and though the winter snow shall pile,
    And leave me chill,
Thy passion's warmth shall make for me, meanwhile,
    A sun-kissed hill.

Invitation to Love

And when the days have lengthened into years,
    And I grow old,
Oh, spite of pains and griefs and cares and fears,
    Grow thou not cold.

Then hand and hand we shall pass up the hill,
    I say not down;
That twain go up, of love, who've loved their fill, -
    To gain love's crown.

Love me, and let my life take up thine own,
    As sun the dew.
Come, sit, my queen, for in my heart a throne
    Awaits for you!

Invitation to Love

Suppose

If 'twere fair to suppose
That your heart were not taken,
That the dew from the rose
Petals still were not shaken,
I should pluck you,
Howe'er you should thorn me and scorn me,
And wear you for life as the green of the bower.

If 'twere fair to suppose
That that road was for vagrants,
That the wind and the rose,
Counted all in their fragrance;
Oh, my dear one,
By love, I should take you and make you,
The green of my life from the scintillant hour.

Love-Song

If Death should claim me for her own to-day,
    And softly I should falter from your side,
Oh, tell me, loved one, would my memory stay,
    And would my image in your heart abide?
Or should I be as some forgotten dream,
    That lives its little space, then fades entire?
Should Time send o'er you its relentless stream,
    To cool your heart, and quench for aye love's fire?

I would not for the world, love, give you pain,
    Or ever compass what would cause you grief;
And, oh, how well I know that tears are vain!
    But love is sweet, my dear, and life is brief;
So if some day before you I should go
    Beyond the sound and sight of song and sea,
'T would give my spirit stronger wings to know
    That you remembered still and wept for me.

Nora: A Serenade.

Ah, Nora, my Nora, the light fades away,
    While Night like a spirit steals up o'er the hills;
The thrush from his tree where he chanted all day,
    No longer his music in ecstasy trills.
Then, Nora, be near me; thy presence doth cheer me,
    Thine eye hath a gleam that is truer than gold.

I cannot but love thee; so do not reprove me,
    If the strength of my passion should make me too bold.
Nora, pride of my heart,—
    Rosy cheeks, cherry lips, sparkling with glee,—
Wake from thy slumbers, wherever thou art;
    Wake from thy slumbers to me.

Ah, Nora, my Nora, there's love in the air,—
    It stirs in the numbers that thrill in my brain;
Oh, sweet, sweet is love with its mingling of care,
    Though joy travels only a step before pain.
Be roused from thy slumbers and list to my numbers;
My heart is poured out in this song unto thee.
Oh, be thou not cruel, thou treasure, thou jewel;
    Turn thine ear to my pleading and hearken to me.

Invitation to Love

Dream Song I

Long years ago, within a distant clime,
Ere Love had touched me with his wand sublime,
I dreamed of one to make my life's calm May
The panting passion of a summer's day.
And ever since, in almost sad suspense,
I have been waiting with a soul intense
To greet and take unto myself the beams,
Of her, my star, the lady of my dreams.

O Love, still longed and looked for, come to me,
Be thy far home by mountain, vale, or sea.
My yearning heart may never find its rest
Until thou liest rapt upon my breast.
The wind may bring its perfume from the south,
Is it so sweet as breath from my love's mouth?
Oh, naught that surely is, and naught that seems
May turn me from the lady of my dreams.

A Bridal Measure

Come, essay a sprightly measure,
Tuned to some light song of pleasure.
Maidens, let your brows be crowned
As we foot this merry round.

From the ground a voice is singing,
From the sod a soul is springing.
Who shall say 't is but a clod
Quick'ning upward toward God?

Who shall say it? Who may know it,
That the clod is not a poet
Waiting but a gleam to waken
In a spirit music-shaken?

Phyllis, Phyllis, why be waiting?
In the woods the birds are mating.
From the tree beside the wall,
Hear the am'rous robin call.

Invitation to Love

Listen to yon thrush's trilling;
Phyllis, Phyllis, are you willing,
When love speaks from cave and tree,
Only we should silent be?

When the year, itself renewing,
All the world with flowers is strewing,
Then through Youth's Arcadian land,
Love and song go hand in hand.

Come, unfold your vocal treasure,
Sing with me a nuptial measure,--
Let this springtime gambol be
Bridal dance for you and me.

The Awakening

I did not know that life could be so sweet,
I did not know the hours could speed so fleet,
Till I knew you, and life was sweet again.
The days grew brief with love and lack of pain—
I was slave a few short days ago,
The powers of Kings and Princes now I know;
I would not be again in bondage, save

Invitation to Love 21

To A Lady Playing The Harp

Thy tones are silver melted into sound,
And as I dream
I see no walls around,
But seem to hear
A gondolier
Sing sweetly down some slow Venetian stream.

Italian skies—that I have never seen—
I see above.
(Ah, play again, my queen;
Thy fingers white
Fly swift and light
And weave for me the golden mesh of love.)

Oh, thou dusk sorceress of the dusky eyes
And soft dark hair,
'T is thou that mak'st my skies
So swift to change
To far and strange;
But far and strange, thou still dost make them fair.

Now thou dost sing, and I am lost in thee
As one who drowns
In floods of melody.
Still in thy art
Give me this part,
Till perfect love, the love of loving crowns.

A Love Song

Ah, love, my love is like a cry in the night,
A long, loud cry to the empty sky,
The cry of a man alone in the desert,
With hands uplifted, with parching lips,

Oh, rescue me, rescue me,
Thy form to mine arms,
The dew of thy lips to my mouth,
Dost thou hear me?—my call thro' the night?

Darling, I hear thee and answer,
Thy fountain am I,
All of the love of my soul will I bring to thee,
All of the pains of my being shall wring to thee,
Deep and forever the song of my loving shall sing to thee,
Ever and ever thro' day and thro' night shall I cling to thee.
Hearest thou the answer?
Darling, I come, I come.

Morning Song Of Love

Darling, my darling, my heart is on the wing,
    It flies to thee this morning like a bird,
Like happy birds in springtime my spirits soar and sing,
    The same sweet song thine ears have often heard.

The sun is in my window, the shadow on the lea,
    The wind is moving in the branches green,
And all my life, my darling, is turning unto thee,
    And kneeling at thy feet, my own, my queen.

The golden bells are ringing across the distant hill,
    Their merry peals come to me soft and clear,
But in my heart's deep chapel all incense-filled and still
    A sweeter bell is sounding for thee, dear.

The bell of love invites thee to come and seek the shrine
    Whose altar is erected unto thee,
The offerings, the sacrifice, the prayers, the chants are thine,
    And I, my love, thy humble priest will be.

Night Of Love

The moon has left the sky, love,
    The stars are hiding now,
And frowning on the world, love,
    Night bares her sable brow.
The snow is on the ground, love,
    And cold and keen the air is.
I 'm singing here to you, love;
    You 're dreaming there in Paris.

But this is Nature's law, love,
    Though just it may not seem,
That men should wake to sing, love,
    While maidens sleep and dream.
Them care may not molest, love,
    Nor stir them from their slumbers,
Though midnight find the swain, love,
    Still halting o'er his numbers.

I watch the rosy dawn, love,
  Come stealing up the east,
While all things round rejoice, love,
  That Night her reign has ceased.
The lark will soon be heard, love,
  And on his way be winging;
When Nature's poets wake, love,
  Why should a man be singing?

Roses And Pearls

Your spoken words are roses fine and sweet,
The songs you sing are perfect pearls of sound.
How lavish nature is about your feet,
To scatter flowers and jewels both around.

Blushing the stream of petal beauty flows,
Softly the white strings trickle down and shine.
Oh! speak to me, my love, I crave a rose.
Sing me a song, for I would pearls were mine.

Come And Kiss Me Sweet And Twenty

Apple blossoms falling o'er thee,
    And the month is May,
Laden bows bend low before thee,
    With their gentle sway;
Look you where the thrush is swinging
    How his melody is ringing,
As he sings my heart is singing:—

    Come and kiss me sweet and twenty,
    Love blooms out with flowers a-plenty,
    Love me, love me without reason,
    Kiss me, now's the kissing season,
    White your cheek is as the blooms are,
    Sweet your breath as perfumes are,
    Is this dolce far niente,
    Come and kiss me sweet and twenty.

Invitation to Love

Love is at thy window suing,
    All the live-long day,
Stay and listen to my wooing,
    Life shall all be May.
Love like mine can falter never
    Naught from thee my heart can sever
And my song shall be forever:—

    Come and kiss me sweet and twenty,
    Love blooms out with flowers a-plenty,
    Love me, love me without reason,
    Kiss me, now's the kissing season,
    White your cheek is as the blooms are,
    Sweet your breath as perfumes are,
    Is this dolce far niente,
    Come and kiss me sweet and twenty.

Invitation to Love

How Shall I Woo Thee

How shall I woo thee to win thee, mine own?
    Say in what tongue shall I tell of my love.
I who was fearless so timid have grown,
    All that was eagle has turned into dove.
The path from the meadow that leads to the bars
Is more to me now than the path of the stars.

How shall I woo thee to win thee, mine own,
    Thou who art fair and as far as the moon?
Had I the strength of the torrent's wild tone,
    Had I the sweetness of warblers in June;
The strength and the sweetness might charm and persuade,
But neither have I my petition to aid.

How shall I woo thee to win thee, mine own?
    How shall I traverse the distance between
My humble cot and your glorious throne?
    How shall a clown gain the ear of a queen?
Oh teach me the tongue that shall please thee the best,
For till I have won thee my heart may not rest.

Invitation to Love

Defining Love

The poems selected for these section take a look at how Dunbar defines love. Many of the poems such as "Kidnapped", "Love Despoiled", "Love Phases", and "The Master-Player" use metaphoric expression to describe love. Many of the poems highlight the innocence of love such as "Her Thoughts and His", "The Quilting", and "Dinah Kneading Dough". Through his writing Dunbar shows us how one sneaks a peak at love and how one tries to understand all of the emotions that love can evoke such as in the poems, "The Disturber", and "Love".

The Master-Player

AN old, worn harp that had been played
Till all its strings were loose and frayed,
Joy, Hate, and Fear, each one essayed,
To play. But each in turn had found
No sweet responsiveness of sound.

Then Love the Master-Player came
With heaving breast and eyes aflame;
The Harp he took all undismayed,
Smote on its strings, still strange to song,
And brought forth music sweet and strong.

A Question

I wist not that I had the pow'r to sing,
But here of late they say my songs are sweet.
Is it because my timid numbers ring
With love's warm music that doth ever beat
Its melody within my throbbing heart?
If so, what else can roguish Cupid do?
I know him master of the archer's art;
Is he a trained musician too?

Invitation to Love

Kidnaped

I held my heart so far from harm,
    I let it wander far and free
In mead and mart, without alarm,
    Assured it must come back to me.

And all went well till on a day,
    Learned Dr. Cupid wandered by
A search along our sylvan way
    For some peculiar butterfly.

A flash of wings, a hurried drive,
    A flutter and a short-lived flit;
This Scientist, as I am alive
    Had seen my heart and captured it.

Right tightly now 'tis held among
The specimens that he has trapped,
And sings (Oh, love is ever young),
    'Tis passing sweet to be kidnaped.

Love

A life was mine full of the close concern
    Of many-voiced affairs. The world sped fast;
    Behind me, ever rolled a pregnant past.
A present came equipped with lore to learn.
Art, science, letters, in their turn,
    Each one allured me with its treasure vast;
    And I staked all for wisdom, till at last
Thou cam'st and taught my soul anew to yearn.
    I had not dreamed that I could turn away
From all that men with brush and pen had wrought;
    But ever since that memorable day
When to my heart the truth of love was brought,
    I have been wholly yielded to its sway,
And had no room for any other thought.

Love Despoiled

As lone I sat one summer's day,
  With mien dejected, Love came by;
His face distraught, his locks astray,
  So slow his gait, so sad his eye,
  I hailed him with a pitying cry:

"Pray, Love, what has disturbed thee so?"
  Said I, amazed. "Thou seem 'st bereft;
And see thy quiver hanging low,—
  What, not a single arrow left?
  Pray, who is guilty of this theft?"

Poor Love looked in my face and cried:
  "No thief were ever yet so bold
To rob my quiver at my side.
  But Time, who rules, gave ear to Gold,
  And all my goodly shafts are sold."

Love's Phases

Love hath the wings of the butterfly,
    Oh, clasp him but gently,
Pausing and dipping and fluttering by
    Inconsequently.
Stir not his poise with the breath of a sigh;
Love hath the wings of the butterfly.

        Love hath the wings of the eagle bold,
           Cling to him strongly—
        What if the look of the world be cold,
           And life go wrongly?
        Rest on his pinions, for broad is their fold;
        Love hath the wings of the eagle bold.

Love hath the voice of the nightingale,
    Hearken his trilling—
List to his song when the moonlight is pale,—
    Passionate, trilling.
Cherish the lay, ere the lilt of it fail;
Love hath the voice of the nightingale.

        Love hath the voice of the storm at night,
           Wildly defiant.
        Hear him and yield up your soul to his might,
           Tenderly pliant.
        None shall regret him who heed him aright;
        Love hath the voice of the storm at night.

A Lyric

My lady love lives far away,
And oh my heart is sad by day,
And ah my tears fall fast by night,
What may I do in such a plight.

Why, miles grow few when love is fleet,
And love, you know, hath flying feet:
Break off thy sighs and witness this,
How poor a thing mere distance is.

My love knows not I love her so,
And would she scorn me, did she know?
How may the tale I would impart
Attract her ear and storm her heart?

        Calm thou the tempest in thy breast,
        Who loves in silence loves the best,
        But bide thy time, she will awake,
        No night so dark but morn will break.

        But tho' my heart so strongly yearn,
        My lady loves me not in turn,
        How may I win the blest reply
        That my void heart shall satisfy.

        Love breedeth love, be thou but true,
        And soon thy Love shall love thee, too;
        If Fate hath meant you heart for heart,
        There's naught may keep you twain apart.

Invitation to Love

The Quilting

Dolly sits a-quilting by her mother,
stitch by stitch,
Gracious, how my pulses throb, how my
fingers itch,
While I note her dainty waist and her slender
hand,
As she matches this and that, she stitches
strand by strand.
And I long to tell her Life's a quilt and I'm
a patch;

Confirmation

He was a poet who wrote clever verses,
And folks said he had fine poetical taste;
But his father, a practical farmer, accused him
Of letting the strength of his arm go to waste.

He called on his sweetheart each Saturday evening,
As pretty a maiden as man ever faced,
And there he confirmed the old man's
 accusation
By letting the strength of his arm go to waist.

The Wooing

A Youth went faring up and down,
    Alack and well-a-day.
He fared him to the market town,
    Alack and well-a-day.
And there he met a maiden fair,
With hazel eyes and auburn hair;
His heart went from him then and there,
    Alack and well-a-day.

She posies sold right merrily,
    Alack and well-a-day;
But not a flower was fair as she,
    Alack and well-a-day.
He bought a rose and sighed a sigh,
"Ah, dearest maiden, would that I
Might dare the seller too to buy!"
    Alack and well-a-day.

She tossed her head, the coy coquette,
    Alack and well-a-day.
"I 'm not, sir, in the market yet,"
    Alack and well-a-day.
"Your love must cool upon a shelf;
Tho' much I sell for gold and pelf,
I 'm yet too young to sell myself,"
    Alack and well-a-day.

The youth was filled with sorrow sore,
    Alack and well-a-day;
And looked he at the maid once more,
    Alack and well-a-day.
Then loud he cried, "Fair maiden, if
Too young to sell, now as I live,
You 're not too young yourself to give,"
    Alack and well-a-day.

The little maid cast down her eyes,
    Alack and well-a-day,
And many a flush began to rise,
    Alack and well-a-day.
"Why, since you are so bold," she said,
"I doubt not you are highly bred,
So take me!" and the twain were wed,
    Alack and well-a-day.

My Little March Girl

Come to the pane, draw the curtain apart,
There she is passing, the girl of my heart;
See where she walks like a queen in the street,
Weather-defying, calm, placid and sweet.
Tripping along with impetuous grace,
Joy of her life beaming out of her face,
Tresses all truant-like, curl upon curl,
Wind-blown and rosy, my little March girl.

Hint of the violet's delicate bloom,
Hint of the rose's pervading perfume!
How can the wind help from kissing her face,—
Wrapping her round in his stormy embrace?
But still serenely she laughs at his rout,
She is the victor who wins the bout.
So may life's passions about her soul swirl,
Leaving it placid,—my little March girl.

What self-possession looks out of her eyes!
What are the wild winds, and what are the skies,
Frowning and glooming when, brimming with life,
Cometh the little maid ripe for the strife?
Ah! Wind, and bah! Wind, what might have you now?
What can you do with that innocent brow?
Blow, Wind, and grow, Wind, and eddy and swirl,
But bring her to me, Wind,—my little March girl.

Her Thought and His

The gray of the sea, and the gray of the sky,
A glimpse of the moon like a half-closed eye.
The gleam on the waves and the light on the land,
A thrill in my heart,-and—my sweetheart's hand.

She turned from the sea with a woman's grace,
And the light fell soft on her upturned face,
And I thought of the flood-tide of infinite bliss
That would flow to my heart from a single kiss.

But my sweetheart was shy, so I dared not ask
For the boon, so bravely I wore the mask.
But into her face there came a flame:—
I wonder could she have been thinking the same?

The Disturber

Oh, what shall I do? I am wholly upset;
I am sure I'll be jailed for a lunatic yet.
I'll be out of a job—it's the thing to expect
When I'm letting my duty go by with neglect.

You may judge the extent and degree of my plight
When I'm thinking all day and a-dreaming all night,
And a-trying my hand at a rhyme on the sly,
All on account of a sparkling eye.

There are those who say men should be strong, well-a-day!
But what constitutes strength in a man? Who shall say?
I am strong as the most when it comes to the arm.
I have aye held my own on the playground or farm.
And when I've been tempted, I have n't been weak;

But now—why, I tremble to hear a maid speak.
I used to be bold, but now I've grown shy,
And all on account of the sparkling eye.

Invitation to Love

There once was a time when my heart was devout,
But now my religion is pen to doubt.
When parson is earnestly preaching of grace,
My fancy is busy with drawing a face,
Thro' the back of a bonnet most piously plain;
'I draw it, redraw it, and draw it again.'
While the songs and the sermon unheeded go by,—
All on account of a sparkling eye.

Oh, dear little conjurer, give o'er your wiles,
It is easy for you, you're all blushes and smiles:
But, love of my heart, I am sorely perplexed;
I am smiling one minute and sighing the next;
And if it goes on, I'll drop hackle and flail,
And go to the parson and tell him my tale.
I warrant he'll find me a cure for the sigh
That you're aye bringing forth with the glance
of your eye.

Invitation to Love

Dinah Kneading Dough

I have seen full many a sight
Born of day or drawn by night:
Sunlight on a silver stream,
Golden lilies all a-dream,
Lofty mountains, bold and proud,
Veiled beneath the lacelike cloud;
But no lovely sight I know
Equals Dinah kneading

    Brown arms buried elbow-deep
    Their domestic rhythm keep,
    As with steady sweep they go
    Through the gently yielding dough.
    Maids may vaunt their finer charms—
    Naught to me like Dinah's arms;
    Girls may draw, or paint, or sew—
    I love Dinah kneading dough.

Eyes of jet and teeth of pearl,
Hair, some say, too tight a-curl;
But the dainty maid I deem
Very near perfection's dream.
Swift she works, and only flings
Me a glance—the least of things.
And I wonder, does she know
That my heart is in the dough?

Invitation to Love

Love's Castle

Key and bar, key and bar,
    Iron bolt and chain!
And what will you do when the King comes
    To enter his domain?

Turn key and lift bar,
    Loose, oh, bolt and chain!
Open the door and let him in,
    And then lock up again.

But, oh, heart, and woe, heart,
    Why do you ache so sore?
Never a moment's peace have you
    Since Love hath passed the door.

Turn key and lift bar,
    And loose bolt and chain;
But Love took in his esquire, Grief,
    And there they both remain.

Love's Seasons

When the bees are humming in the honeysuckle vine
    And the summer days are in their bloom,
Then my love is deepest, oh, dearest heart of mine,
When the bees are humming in the honeysuckle vine.

When the winds are moaning o'er the meadows chill and gray,
    And the land is dim with winter gloom,
Then for thee, my darling, love will have its way,
When the winds are moaning o'er the meadows chill and gray.

In the vernal dawning with the starting of the leaf,
    In the merry-chanting time of spring,
Love steals all my senses, oh, the happy-hearted thief!
In the vernal morning with the starting of the leaf.

Always, ever always, even in the autumn drear,
    When the days are sighing out their grief,
Thou art still my darling, dearest of the dear,
Always, ever always, even in the autumn drear.

Two Songs

A bee that was searching for sweets one day
Through the gate of a rose garden happened to stray.
In the heart of a rose he hid away,
And forgot in his bliss the light of day,
As sipping his honey he buzzed in song;
Though day was waning, he lingered long,
  For the rose was sweet, so sweet.

A robin sits pluming his ruddy breast,
And a madrigal sings to his love in her nest:
"Oh, the skies they are blue, the fields are green,
And the birds in your nest will soon be seen!"
She hangs on his words with a thrill of love,
And chirps to him as he sits above
  For the song is sweet, so sweet.

A maiden was out on a summer's day
With the winds and the waves and the flowers at play;
And she met with a youth of gentle air,
With the light of the sunshine on his hair.
Together they wandered the flowers among;
They loved, and loving they lingered long,
  For to love is sweet, so sweet.

Passion And Love

A maiden wept and, as a comforter,
Came one who cried, "I love thee," and he seized
Her in his arms and kissed her with hot breath,
That dried the tears upon her flaming cheeks.
While evermore his boldly blazing eye
Burned into hers; but she uncomforted
Shrank from his arms and only wept the more.

Then one came and gazed mutely in her face
With wide and wistful eyes; but still aloof
He held himself; as with a reverent fear,
As one who knows some sacred presence nigh.
And as she wept he mingled tear with tear,
That cheered her soul like dew a dusty flower,—
Until she smiled, approached, and touched his hand!

Invitation to Love

Losing Love

Dunbar shares the pain of losing love through the poems in this section. "My Love Irene", "Ships That Pass In The Night", and "Lyrics of Love and Sorrow" are a few that express the emotional pain that one can feel when hurt by love. One of the best poems in this section is, "If I Could but Forget". It should be considered a classic.

My Love Irene

Farewell, farewell, my love Irene;
The pangs of sadness stir my breast;
Though many miles may intervene,
My soul's with thine, in East or West.
Go where thou wilt, to wealth or fame;
Win for thyself or praise or blame,
My love shall ever be the same,
My love Irene.

    Farewell, farewell, my love Irene;
    Oh, sad decree, that we must part!
    The wound is deep, the pain is keen
    That agitates mine aching heart.
    My feverish eyes burn up their tears;
    I cannot still my doubts and fears;
    And this one sigh the night wind hears,
    My love Irene.

        Farewell, farewell, my love Irene;
        The morning's gray now floods the sky;
        The sun peeps from his misty screen;
        Mine only love, good-bye, good-bye.
        All love must fade, all life must die,
        The smile must turn into the sigh.
        Alas! how hard to say good-bye,
        My love Irene.

Ballard

I KNOW my love is true,
   And oh the day is fair.
The sky is clear and blue,
The flowers are rich of hue,
    The air I breathe is rare,
   I have no grief or care;
For my own love is true,
   And oh the day is fair.

My love is false I find,
   And oh the day is dark.
Blows sadly down the wind,
While sorrow holds my mind;
    I do not hear the lark,
    For quenched is life's dear spark,--
My love is false I find,
   And oh the day is dark!

For love doth make the day
   Or dark or doubly bright;
Her beams along the way
Dispel the gloom and gray.
   She lives and all is bright,
   She dies and life is night.
For love doth make the day,
   Or dark or doubly bright.

Invitation to Love

Ships That Pass In The Night

Out in the sky the great dark clouds are massing;
   I look far out into the pregnant night,
Where I can hear a solemn booming gun
   And catch the gleaming of a random light,
That tells me that the ship I seek is passing, passing.

My tearful eyes my soul's deep hurt are glassing;
   For I would hail and check that ship of ships.
I stretch my hands imploring, cry aloud,
   My voice falls dead a foot from mine own lips
And but its ghost doth reach that vessel, passing, passing.

O Earth, O Sky, O Ocean, both surpassing,
   O heart of mine, O soul that dreads the dark!
Is there no hope for me? Is there no way
   That I may sight and check that speeding bark
Which out of sight and sound is passing, passing?

Lyrics Of Love And Sorrow

I

Love is the light of the world, my dear,
  Heigho, but the world is gloomy;
The light has failed and the lamp down hurled,
  Leaves only darkness to me.

Love is the light of the world, my dear,
  Ah me, but the world is dreary;
The night is down, and my curtain furled
  But I cannot sleep, though weary.

Love is the light of the world, my dear,
  Alas for a hopeless hoping,
When the flame went out in the breeze that swirled,
  And a soul went blindly groping.

II

The light was on the golden sands,
  A glimmer on the sea;
My soul spoke clearly to thy soul,
  Thy spirit answered me.

I Since then the light that gilds the sands,
  And glimmers on the sea,
But vainly struggles to reflect
  The radiant soul of thee.

II
  The sea speaks to me of you
    All the day long;
  Still as I sit by its side
    You are its song.

  The sea sings to me of you
    Loud on the reef;
  Always it moans as it sings,
    Voicing my grief.

IV
  My dear love died last night;
    Shall I clothe her in white?
  My passionate love is dead,
    Shall I robe her in red?
  But nay, she was all untrue,
    She shall not go drest in blue;
  Still my desolate love was brave,

V

There are brilliant heights of sorrow
  That only the few may know;
And the lesser woes of the world, like waves,
  Break noiselessly, far below.
I hold for my own possessing,
  A mount that is lone and still—
The great high place of a hopeless grief,
  And I call it my "Heart-break Hill."
And once on a winter's midnight
  I found its highest crown,
And there in the gloom, my soul and I,
  Weeping, we sat us down.

But now when I seek that summit
  We are two ghosts that go;
Only two shades of a thing that died,
  Once in the long ago.
So I sit me down in the silence,
  And say to my soul, "Be still,"
So the world may not know we died that night,
  From weeping on "Heart-break Hill."

Invitation to Love

Love's Draft

The draft of love was cool and sweet
    You gave me in the cup,
But, ah, love's fire is keen and fleet,
    And I am burning up.

Unless the tears I shed for you
    Shall quench this burning flame,
It will consume me through and through,
    And leave but ash—a name.

A Golden Day

I found you and I lost you,
All on a gleaming day.
The day was filled with sunshine,
And the land was full of May.

A golden bird was singing
Its melody divine,
I found you and I loved you,
And all the world was mine.

I found you and I lost you,
All on a golden day,
But when I dream of you, dear,
It is always brimming May.

Then and Now

Then.
He loved her and through many years,
Had paid his fair devoted court,
Until she wearied and with sneers
Turned all his ardent love to sport.
That night within his chamber lone,
He long sat writing by his bed
A note in which his heart made moan
For love the morning found him dead.

Now.
Like him a man of later day
Was jilted by the maid he sought,
And from her presence turned away,
Consumed by burning, bitter thought.
He sought his room to write—a curse
Like him before and die, I ween.
Ah no, he put his woes in verse,
And sold them to a magazine.

Yesterday And To-Morrow

Yesterday I held your hand,
Reverently I pressed it,
And its gentle yieldingness
From my soul I blessed it.

But to-day I sit alone,
Sad and sore repining;
Must our gold forever know
Flames for the refining?

Yesterday I walked with you,
Could a day be sweeter?
Life was all a lyric song
Set to tricksy meter.

   Ah, to-day is like a dirge,—
   Place my arms around you,
   Let me feel the same dear joy
   As when first I found you.

   Let me once retrace my steps,
   From these roads unpleasant,
   Let my heart and mind and soul
   All ignore the present.

   Yesterday the iron seared
   And to-day means sorrow.
   Pause, my soul, arise, arise,
   Look where gleams the mor-

Love And Grief

Out of my heart, one treach'rous winter's day,
I locked young Love and threw the key away.
Grief, wandering widely, found the key,
And hastened with it, straightway, back to me,
With Love beside him. He unlocked the door
And bad Love enter with him there and stay.
And so the twain abide for evermore.

Love's Chastening.

Once Love grew bold and arrogant of air,
Proud of the youth that made him fresh and fair;
So unto Grief he spake, "What right hast thou
To part or parcel of this heart?" Grief's brow
Was darkened with the storm of inward strife;
Thrice smote he Love as only he might dare,
And Love, pride purged, was chastened all his life.

If I Could but Forget

If I could but forget
The fullness of those first sweet days,
When you burst sun-like thro' the haze
Of unacquaintance, on my sight,
And made the wet, gray day seem bright
While clouds themselves grew fair to see.
    And since, no day is gray or wet,
But all the scene comes back to me,
    If I could but forget.

        If I could but forget
        How your dusk eyes look into mine,
        And how I thrilled as with strong wine
        Beneath your touch; while sped amain
        The quickened stream thro' ev'ry vein;
        How near my breath fell to a gasp,
            When for a space our fingers met
        In one electric vibrant clasp,
            If I could but forget.

If I could but forget
The months of passion and of pain,
And all that followed in their train—
Rebellious thoughts that would arise,
Rebellious tears that dimmed mine eyes,
The prayers that I might set love's fire
    Aflame within your bosom yet—
The death at last of that desire—
    If I could but forget.

Invitation to Love

Humorous Love

Sometimes love can make us laugh at ourselves. Love can cause us to think silly thoughts, act in funny ways, and use all of our energy to made our love known. The poems written in this section present the humorous side of love. Many of the poems are written in black dialect, the writing form in which Dunbar was most known. One of Dunbar's most famous poems, "A Negro Love Song" is included in this section. Less known poems such as "A Made to Order Smile", "The Photograph", "Discovered", and "A Love Letter" are also true gems.

A Made to Order Smile

When a woman looks up at you with a twist about her eyes,
And her brows are half uplifted in a nicely feigned surprise
As you breathe some pretty sentence,
   though she hates you all the while,
She is very apt to stun you with a made to order smile.

It's a subtle combination of a sneer and a caress,
With a dash of warmth thrown in it to relieve its iciness,
And she greets you when she meets you with that look as if a file
Had been used to fix and fashion out that made to order smile.

I confess that I'm eccentric and am not a woman's man,
For they seem to be constructed on the bunko fakir plan,
And it somehow sets me thinking that her heart is full of guile
When a woman looks up at me with a made to order smile.

Now, all maidens, young and aged, hear the lesson I would teach--
Ye who meet us in the ballroom, ye who meet us at the beach--
Pray consent to try and charm us by some other sort of wile
And relieve us from the burden of that made to order smile.

A Negro Love Song

Seen my lady home las' night,
    Jump back, honey, jump back.
Hel' huh han' an' sque'z it tight,
    Jump back, honey, jump back.
Hyeahd huh sigh a little sigh,
Seen a light gleam f'om huh eye,
An' a smile go flittin' by
    Jump back, honey, jump back.

Hyeahd de win' blow thoo de pine,
    Jump back, honey, jump back.
Mockin'-bird was singin' fine,
    Jump back, honey, jump back.
An' my hea't was beatin' so,
When I reached my lady's do',
Dat I could n't ba' to go—
    Jump back, honey, jump back.

Put my ahm aroun' huh wais',
    Jump back, honey, jump back.
Raised huh lips an' took a tase,
    Jump back, honey, jump back.
Love me, honey, love me true?
Love me well ez I love you?
An' she answe'd, "'Cose I do"
    Jump back, honey, jump back.

Invitation to Love

The Photograph

See dis pictyah in my han'?
    Dat's my gal;
Ain't she purty? goodness lan'!
    Huh name Sal.
Dat's de very way she be --
Kin' o' tickles me to see
Huh a-smilin' back at me.

        She sont me dis photygraph
           Jes' las' week;
        An' aldough hit made me laugh --
           My black cheek
        Felt somethin' a-runnin' queer;
        Bless yo' soul, it was a tear
        Jes' f''om wishin' she was here.

Often when I 's all alone
    Layin' here,
I git t'inkin' bout my own
    Sallie dear;
How she say dat I 's huh beau,
An' hit tickles me to know
Dat de gal do love me so.

        Some bright day I 's goin' back,
           Fo' de la!
        An' ez sho' 's my face is black,
           Ax huh pa
        Fu' de blessed little miss
        Who 's a-smiling' out o' dis
        Pictyah, lak she wan'ed a kiss!

Invitation to Love

Discovered

SEEN you down at chu'ch las' night,
    Nevah min', Miss Lucy.
What I mean? oh, dat 's all right,
    Nevah min', Miss Lucy.
You was sma't ez sma't could be,
But you could n't hide f'om me.
Ain't I got two eyes to see!
    Nevah min', Miss Lucy.

Guess you thought you 's awful keen;
    Nevah min', Miss Lucy.
Evahthing you done, I seen;
    Nevah min', Miss Lucy.
Seen him tek yo' ahm jes' so,
When he got outside de do' —
Oh, I know dat man's yo' beau!
    Nevah min', Miss Lucy.

Say now, honey, wha'd he say? —
    Nevah min', Miss Lucy!
Keep yo' secrets — dat 's yo' way —
    Nevah min', Miss Lucy.
Won't tell me an' I 'm yo' pal —
I 'm gwine tell his othah gal, —
Know huh, too, huh name is Sal;
    Nevah min', Miss Lucy!

Invitation to Love

A Love Letter

OH, I des received a letter f'om de sweetes' little gal;
    Oh, my; oh, my.
She's my lovely little sweethaht an' her name is Sal:
    Oh, my; oh, my.
She writes me dat she loves me an' she loves me true,
She wonders ef I'll tell huh dat I loves huh, too;
An' my h'aht's so full o' music dat I do' know what to do;
    Oh, my; oh, my.

I got a man to read it an' he read it fine;
    Oh, my; oh, my.
Dey ain' no use denyin' dat her love is mine;
    Oh, my; oh, my.
But hyeah's de t'ing dat's puttin' me in such a awful plight,
I t'ink of huh at mornin' an' I dream of huh at night;
But how's I gwine to cou't huh w'en I do' know how to write?
    Oh, my; oh, my.

My h'aht is bubblin' ovah wid de t'ings I want to say;
    Oh, my; oh, my.
An' dey's lots of folks to copy what I tell 'em fu' de pay;
    Oh, my; oh, my.
But dey's t'ings dat I's a-t'inkin' dat is only fu' huh eahs,
An' I could n't lu'n to write 'em ef I took a dozen yeahs;
So to go down daih an' tell huh is de only way, it 'peahs;
    Oh, my; oh, my.

Angelina

W'EN de fiddle gits to singin' out a ol' Vahginny reel,
An' you 'mence to feel a ticklin' in yo' toe an' in yo' heel;
Ef you t'ink you got 'uligion an' you wants to keep it, too,
You jes' bettah tek a hint an' git yo'se'f clean out o' view.
Case de time is mighty temptin' w'en de chune is in de swing,
Fu' a darky, saint or sinner man, to cut de pigeon-wing.
An' you could n't he'p f'om dancin' ef yo' feet was boun' wif twine,
W'en Angelina Johnson comes a-swingin' down de line.

Don't you know Miss Angelina? She's de da'lin' of de place.
W'y, dey ain't no high-toned lady wif sich mannahs an' sich grace.
She kin move across de cabin, wif its planks all rough an' wo';
Jes' de same's ef she was dancin' on ol' mistus' ball-room flo'.
Fact is, you do' see no cabin--evah- t'ing you see look gran',
An' dat one ol' squeaky fiddle soun' to you jes' lak a ban';
Cotton britches look lak broadclof an' a linsey dress look fine,
W'en Angelina Johnson comes a-swingin' down de line.

Some folks say dat dancin's sinful, an' de blessed Lawd, dey say,
Gwine to purnish us fu' steppin' w'en we hyeah de music play.
But I tell you I don' b'lieve it, fu' de Lawd is wise and good,
An' he made de banjo's metal an' he made de fiddle's wood,
An' he made de music in dem, so I don' quite t'ink he'll keer
Ef our feet keeps time a little to de melodies we hyeah.
W'y, dey's somep'n' downright holy in de way our faces shine,
W'en Angelina Johnson comes a-swingin' down de line.

Angelina step' so gentle, Angelina bow' so low,
An' she lif' huh sku't so dainty dat huh shoetop skacely show:
An' dem teef o' huh'n a-shinin', ez she tek you by de han'--
Go 'way, people, d' ain't anothah sich a lady in de lan'!
W'en she's movin' thoo de figgers er a-dancin' by huhse'f,
Folks jes' stan' stock-still a-sta'in', an' dey mos' nigh hol's dey bref;
An' de young mens, dey's a-sayin', "I's gwine mek dat damsel mine,"
W'en Angelina Johnson comes a-swingin' down de line.

Invitation to Love

Parted

DE breeze is blowin' 'cross de bay,
   My lady, my lady;
De ship hit teks me far away,
   My lady, my lady.
Ole Mas' done sol' me down de stream;
Dey tell me 't ain't so bad 's hit seem,
   My lady, my lady.

O' co'se I knows dat you 'll be true,
   My lady, my lady;
But den I do' know whut to do,
   My lady, my lady.
I knowed some day we 'd have to pa't,
But den hit put' nigh breaks my hea't,
   My lady, my lady.

De day is long, de night is black,
   My lady, my lady;
I know you 'll wait twell I come back,
   My lady, my lady.
I 'll stan' de ship, I 'll stan' de chain,
But I 'll come back, my darlin' Jane,
   My lady, my lady.

Jes' wait, jes' b'lieve in whut I say,
   My lady, my lady;
D' ain t nothin' dat kin keep me 'way,
   My lady, my lady.
A man 's a man, an' love is love;
God knows ouah hea'ts, my little dove;
He 'll he'p us f''om his th'one above,

Invitation to Love

The Looking-Glass

Dinah stan' befo' de glass,
    Lookin' moughty neat,
An' huh purty shadder sass
    At huh haid an' feet.
While she sasshay 'roun' an' bow,
Smilin' den an' poutin' now,
An' de lookin'-glass, I 'low,
    Say: "Now, ain't she sweet?"

All she do, de glass it see,
    Hit des see, no mo',
Seems to me, hit ought to be
    Drappin' on de flo'.
She go w'en huh time git slack,
Kissin' han's an' smilin' back,
Lawsy, how my lips go smack,
    Watchin' at de do'.

Wisht I was huh lookin'-glass,
    Wen she kissed huh han';
Does you t'ink I 'd let it pass,
    Settin' on de stan'?
No; I'd des' fall down an' break,
Kin' o' glad 't uz fu' huh sake;
But de diffunce, dat whut make
    Lookin'-glass an' man.

Invitation to Love

A Plea

Treat me nice, Miss Mandy Jane,
   Treat me nice.
Dough my love has tu'ned my brain,
   Treat me nice.
I ain't done a t'ing to shame,
Lovahs all ac's jes' de same;
Don't you know we ain't to blame?
   Treat me nice!

                      Cose I know I 's talkin' wild;
                           Treat me nice;
                      I cain't talk no bettah, child,
                           Treat me nice;
                      Whut a pusson gwine to do,
                      Wen he come a-cou'tin' you
                      All a-trimblin' thoo and thoo?
                         Please be nice.

Reckon I mus' go de paf
   Othahs do:
Lovahs lingah, ladies laff;
   Mebbe you
Do' mean all the things you say,
An' pu'haps some latah day
W'en I baig you ha'd, you may
   Treat me nice!

Invitation to Love

Howdy Honey Howdy

Do' a-stan'in' on a jar, fiah a-shinin' thoo,
Ol' folks drowsin' 'roun' de place, wide awake is Lou,
W'en I tap, she answah, an' I see huh 'mence to grin,
"Howdy, honey, howdy, won't you step right in?"

Den I step erpon de log layin' at de do',
Bless de Lawd, huh mammy an' huh pap's done 'menced to sno',
Now's de time, if evah, ef I's gwine to try an' win,
"Howdy, honey, howdy, won't you step right in?"

No use playin' on de aidge, trimblin' on de brink,
W'en a body love a gal, tell huh whut he t'ink;
W'en huh hea't is open fu' de love you gwine to gin,
Pull yo'se'f togethah, suh, an' step right in.

Sweetes' imbitation dat a body evah hyeahed,
Sweetah den de music of a love-sick mockin'-bird,
Comin' f'om de gal you loves bettah den yo' kin,
"Howdy, honey, howdy, won't you step right in?"

At de gate o' heaven w'en de sto'm o' life is pas',
'Spec' I'll be a-stan'in', 'twell de Mastah say at las',
"Hyeah he stan' all weary, but he winned his fight wid sin.
Howdy, honey, howdy, won't you step right in? "

Invitation to Love

My Sweet Brown Gal

W'en de clouds is hangin' heavy in de sky,
An' de win's 's a-taihin' moughty vig'rous by,
I don' go a-sighin' all erlong de way;
I des' wo'k a-waitin' fu' de close o' day.

Case I knows w'en evenin' draps huh shadders down,
I won' care a smidgeon fu' de weathah's frown;
Let de rain go splashin', let de thundah raih,
Dey 's a happy sheltah, an' I 's goin' daih.

Down in my ol' cabin wa'm ez mammy's toas',
'Taters in de fiah layin' daih to roas';
No one daih to cross me, got no talkin' pal,
But I 's got de comp'ny o' my sweet brown gal.

So I spen's my evenin' listenin' to huh sing,
Lak a blessid angel; how huh voice do ring!
Sweetah den a bluebird flutterin' erroun',
W'en he sees de steamin' o' de new ploughed groun'.

Den I hugs huh closah, closah to my breas'.
Need n't sing, my da'lin', tek you' hones' res'.
Does I mean Malindy, Mandy, Lize er Sal?
No, I means my fiddle—dat's my sweet brown gal!

Invitation to Love

Bibliography

Braxton, Joanne M., ed. <u>The Collected Poetry of Paul Laurence Dunbar.</u> Charlottesville: University Press of Virginia, 1993.

Cunningham, Virginia. <u>Paul Laurence Dunbar and His Song.</u> New York: Dodd, Mead & Company, 1947.

Dunbar, Alice, et al. <u>Paul Laurence Dunbar: Poet Laureate of the Negro Race.</u> Philadelphia: A.M.E. Church Review, 1914.

Dunbar, Paul Laurence. <u>The Complete Poems of Paul Laurence Dunbar.</u> With an introduction to Lyrics of Lowly Life by W. D. Howells. Howells : William Dean New York : Dodd, Mead, 1913 (reprints from 1913-1952).

Gayle, Addison Jr. <u>Oak and Ivy: A Biography of Paul Laurence Dunbar.</u> New York: Doubleday, 1971.

Paul Laurence Dunbar Digital Collection. January, 2006. Wright State University Libraries. 1 Jan. 2007. <http://www.libraries.wright.edu/special/dunbar>.

Paul Laurence Dunbar Website. February, 2003. University of Dayton. 1 Jan. 2007. <http://www.plethoreum.org/dunbar>.

Sci, Laverne. Personal Interview. 15 Nov. 1996.

About the Author

Dr. Rhonda Rhea, serves as an advisor and confidant to a number of non-profit, educational and religious entities in the areas of compliance and policy. She holds a Juris Doctorate Degree from Howard University School of Law; a Master of Divinity Degree from Howard University School of Divinity; and a Bachelor of Art Degree in Mass Media Arts from Hampton University.

A commissioned writer and professional advocate, Dr. Rhea has written poetry, plays and short stories since childhood. In recent years, Dr. Rhea has concentrated on historical research projects that highlight the achievements of African Americans. In addition to this project, Dr. Rhea is currently working on two museum exhibits. It is her desire to raise an awareness of the many accomplishments of unsung individuals.

Dr. Rhea is a member of many organizations including Alpha Kappa Alpha Sorority, Incorporated and Jack and Jill of America, Inc. A dynamic spiritual and motivational speaker, Dr. Rhea offers insight and encouragement to her audiences.